MARKS &
SPENCER

bread

simple and delicious easy-to-make
recipes for your bread maker

Linda Doeser

Marks and Spencer p.l.c.
Baker Street, London, W1U 8EP

www.marksandspencer.com

ISBN: 1-84273-868-2

Printed in China

Produced by the Bridgewater Book Company Ltd

Photographer Calvey Taylor-Haw

Home Economist Michaela Jester

All the recipes in this book are for use with a bread machine

NOTES FOR THE READER

- Always read the bread machine manufacturer's handbook. Although most bread machines work in basically the same way, there are some important variations from brand to brand.

- Add the ingredients in the order given in the ingredients list unless the instructions require you to add the dry ingredients first. In that case, simply reverse the order. Measure ingredients accurately. Do not mix the imperial and metric measures. All spoon measurements are level: teaspoons are assumed to be 5 ml and tablespoons are assumed to be 15 ml.

- Make sure that the kneading blade is properly attached. Do not plug the machine in until you are ready to switch it on. Always remove the bread pan to add the ingredients to avoid spills inside the machine.

- Ingredients should be at room temperature first. Use hand-hot liquid – but no hotter – as this will activate the yeast. Make sure that flours and yeast are not past their 'use-by' dates.

- Do not open the bread machine during cooking, except when necessary for adding extra ingredients. Otherwise, the temperature will drop and the bread will be disappointing.

- Use oven gloves to remove the bread pan after baking – it will be very hot. Make sure the bread machine is on a level surface and cannot be reached by young children.

- Do not use the timer delay for recipes that include perishable ingredients, such as eggs, yogurt or buttermilk.

- The recipes in this book have been tested in medium-sized machines. They are all suitable for large machines and most will work successfully in small machines. Check the manufacturer's handbook for maximum capacity.

- For shaped loaves, follow the instructions for proving the dough (letting it rise). Place in a warm place, such as an airing cupboard. The dough may take longer to rise in a cooler place. Always preheat the oven fully before baking.

contents

introduction

There can be few more appetising aromas than the smell of bread baking and few more delicious tastes than a still-warm, freshly cooked loaf. With a bread machine, this can quickly become a trouble-free, everyday treat. If you have a timer delay, fresh bread every morning is even less trouble than brewing a pot of coffee.

The recipes in this book cover all kinds of bread for every occasion and lifestyle. There are simple, basic breads that require no more effort than measuring a few ingredients into the machine and pressing the start switch, yet even these provide a wide range of flavours, from a plain white loaf to a moist fruit bread. More ambitious cooks can use the machine to take the hard work out of making the dough, and create professional-looking plaits, baguettes, baps, breadsticks and Danish pastries. The versatility of the bread machine is further explored with mouthwatering pizza recipes as well as some fabulous cakes to perk up mid-morning coffee or afternoon tea.

Bread, in one form or another, features in the diets of every country in the world. The recipes in this book include a global round-up of French, Italian, Finnish, Indian, Hungarian, Austrian, Danish, Caribbean, Scottish and American specialities, as well as traditional English treats, such as Cornish Saffron Bread and Devonshire Splits.

guide to recipe key		
	very easy	Recipes are graded as follows: 1 pea = easy; 2 peas = very easy; 3 peas = extremely easy.
	1 small loaf	Recipes generally make a small or medium loaf, or the quantity is specified: e.g. two 25-cm/10-inch pizzas.
	25 minutes	Hands-on preparation time for machine-only breads. For machine-prepared and oven-baked recipes, the time the dough spends in the machine is also included.
	3 hours	The overall time spent in the machine for machine-only breads, or the baking time in the oven for recipes where the dough is prepared in the machine first.

The kneading paddle should be well seated in the bottom of the bread pan.

Make sure that you add the ingredients in the order given by the recipe.

Sit the bread pan securely inside the bread machine before closing the lid.

When the bread has baked, remove it from the bread pan to allow it to cool.

family
favourites

Here are some easy recipes for a wide range of different loaves. For the simplest, you just place all of the ingredients in the machine, press start, and turn out a perfect loaf to cool. Varying the ingredients produces a delicious selection of breads, from Wholemeal Harvest Bread to American Corn Bread. There are also popular breads and rolls for cooking in a conventional oven. Use the bread machine to make perfect dough, then turn out and shape. You will find that more specialist loaves, such as Poppy Seed Plait and French Baguettes, are well within the scope of the beginner.

crusty white bread

		ingredients	
	extremely easy	1 egg	1½ tsp salt
		1 egg yolk	2 tsp sugar
	1 medium loaf	hand-hot water, as required	25 g /1 oz butter, softened or diced
		500 g/1 lb 2 oz strong white bread flour	1 tsp easy-blend dried yeast
	10 minutes		
	about 3 hours		

Put the egg and egg yolk into a measuring jug and beat lightly to mix. Add sufficient hand-hot water to make up to 300 ml/10 fl oz. Stir to mix then pour into the bread pan.

Sprinkle the flour over the liquid to cover. Place the salt, sugar and butter in 3 corners of the pan. Indent the flour without exposing the liquid and add the yeast.

Set the bread machine to the basic setting, medium crust, and press start.

When the cycle has finished, turn out the bread to cool.

wholemeal harvest bread

		ingredients	
extremely easy	175 ml/6 fl oz hand-hot water	1 tsp salt	
	1½ tbsp sunflower oil	2 tbsp soft brown sugar	
1 small loaf	225 g/8 oz strong wholemeal bread flour	1 tsp easy-blend dried yeast	
5 minutes	1 tbsp skimmed milk powder		
about 3½ hours			

Pour the water into the bread pan and add the sunflower oil.

Sprinkle the flour over the liquid to cover, then sprinkle in the skimmed milk powder. Place the salt and sugar in 2 corners of the pan. Indent the flour without exposing the liquid and add the yeast.

Set the bread machine to the wholemeal setting, medium crust, and press start.

When the cycle has finished, turn out the bread to cool.

milk loaf

		ingredients	
extremely easy		200 ml/7 fl oz hand-hot full cream or semi-skimmed milk	1½ tsp salt
			2 tsp sugar
1 medium loaf		100 ml/3½ fl oz hand-hot water	25 g/1 oz butter, softened or diced
		450 g/1 lb strong white bread flour	1 tsp easy-blend dried yeast
5 minutes			
about 3 hours			

Pour the milk and water into the bread pan.

Sprinkle the flour over the liquid to cover. Place the salt, sugar and butter in 3 corners of the pan. Indent the flour without exposing the liquid and add the yeast.

Set the bread machine to the basic setting, medium crust, and press start.

When the cycle has finished, turn out the bread to cool.

poppy seed plait

		ingredients
easy	175 ml/6 fl oz hand-hot water	TOPPING
	2 tbsp sunflower oil, plus extra	1 egg yolk
1 loaf	for greasing	1 tbsp milk
	225 g/8 oz strong white bread flour,	1 tbsp caster sugar
	plus extra for dusting	2 tbsp poppy seeds
2¼ hours	2 tbsp skimmed milk powder	
	1 tsp salt	
	1½ tbsp sugar	
30–35 minutes	1 tsp easy-blend dried yeast	
	3 tbsp poppy seeds	

Pour the water into the bread pan and add the sunflower oil. Sprinkle the flour over the liquid to cover, then add the skimmed milk powder. Place the salt and sugar in 2 corners of the pan. Indent the flour without exposing the liquid and add the yeast.

Set the bread machine to the dough setting and press start. Five minutes before the end, add the poppy seeds. Remove the finished dough from the pan. Knock back gently on a floured surface and knead lightly. Divide into 3 equal pieces and shape each piece into a rope. Plait the ropes, pinch them together at each end and tuck under. Place on an oiled baking sheet, cover with clingfilm, and set aside in a warm place to rise for 30 minutes.

For the topping, lightly beat the egg yolk with the milk and sugar. Remove the clingfilm and brush over the loaf, then sprinkle over the poppy seeds. Bake in a preheated oven, 200°C/400°F/Gas Mark 6, for 30–35 minutes, until golden. Turn out the bread to cool.

french baguettes

		ingredients	
easy		325 ml/11 fl oz hand-hot water	1½ tsp salt
		450 g/1 lb strong white bread flour,	1½ tsp easy-blend dried yeast
2 loaves		plus extra for dusting	sunflower oil, for greasing
4 hours			
15–20 minutes			

Pour the water into the bread pan. Sprinkle the flour over the liquid to cover. Place the salt in a corner of the pan. Indent the flour without exposing the liquid and add the yeast. Set the machine to French dough setting and press start.

Remove the finished dough from the pan. Knock back on a lightly floured surface, then divide in half. Shape each piece into a ball then roll out into 2 rectangles. With the long sides facing, fold the top third of each rectangle down and the bottom third up and press together. Repeat twice more with each rectangle, resting the dough in between each folding. Gently roll and stretch each piece of dough, in turn, into a stick about 30 cm/12 inches long.

Place between the folds of a pleated tea towel for support and cover with oiled clingfilm. Set aside in a warm place for 30–40 minutes to rise. Remove the clingfilm. Slash the tops. Dampen the inside of a preheated oven, 230°C/450°F/Gas Mark 8. Bake for 15–20 minutes.

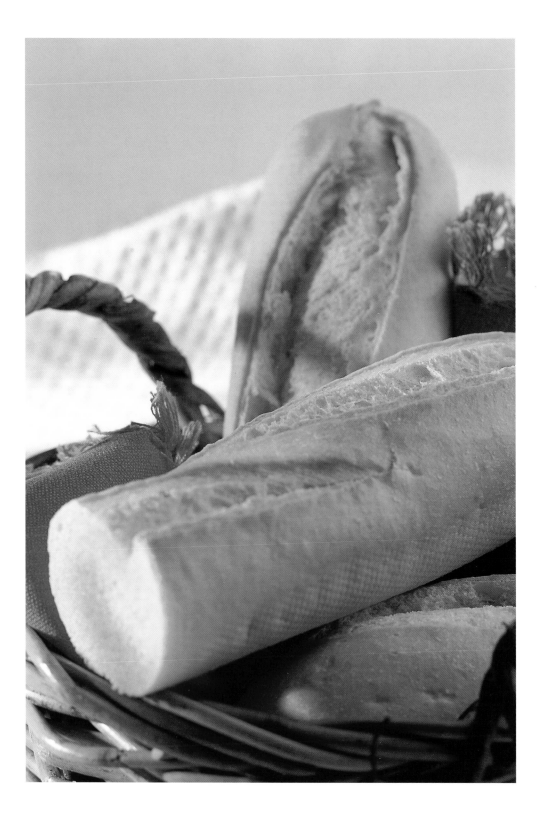

potato & oatmeal bread

		ingredients	
very easy	225 g/8 oz floury potatoes (peeled weight)		1½ tbsp dark brown sugar 40 g/1½ oz butter, softened or diced
1 medium loaf	210 ml/7½ fl oz hand-hot water 500 g/1 lb 2 oz strong white bread flour		1½ tsp easy-blend dried yeast TOPPING
40 minutes	3 tbsp rolled oats 2 tbsp skimmed milk powder 1½ tsp salt		1 tbsp water 1 tbsp rolled oats
about 3 hours			

Place the potatoes in a pan, add water to cover, bring to the boil and cook for 20–25 minutes, until tender. Drain and mash until smooth. Set aside to cool.

Pour the water into the bread pan. Sprinkle the flour over the liquid to cover, then sprinkle in the rolled oats and skimmed milk powder. Add the mashed potatoes to the bread pan, then place the salt, sugar and butter in 3 corners of the pan. Indent the flour without exposing the liquid and add the yeast.

Set the bread machine to the basic setting, medium crust, and press start. About 5 minutes before the end of the final rising cycle (about 1¼ hours from the start), add the topping. Brush the top of the loaf with the water and carefully sprinkle over the rolled oats.

When the cycle has finished, turn out the bread to cool.

pitta breads

		ingredients	
very easy		210 ml/7½ fl oz hand-hot water	1 tsp sugar
		350 g/12 oz strong white bread flour,	1 tsp easy-blend dried yeast
6 pittas		plus extra for dusting	1 tbsp olive oil, plus extra for greasing
		1½ tsp salt	
2 hours			
5 minutes			

Pour the water into the bread pan. Sprinkle the flour over the liquid to cover. Place the salt and sugar in 2 corners of the pan. Indent the flour without exposing the liquid. Add the yeast and the oil. Set the bread machine to the pizza dough setting and press start.

Remove the finished dough from the bread pan. Knock back gently on a lightly floured surface, then divide into 6 equal pieces. Shape each piece into a ball and place on a tray. Cover with oiled clingfilm and set aside for 10 minutes. Meanwhile, place 2–3 baking sheets in the oven and preheat to 230°C/450°F/Gas Mark 8.

Uncover the dough and flatten each piece slightly. Roll out each piece into a round. Sprinkle lightly with flour and cover with oiled clingfilm. Set aside for 10 minutes to rest. Remove the clingfilm and transfer the rounds to the baking sheets, spaced well apart. Bake for 5 minutes, until risen and golden. Turn out to cool.

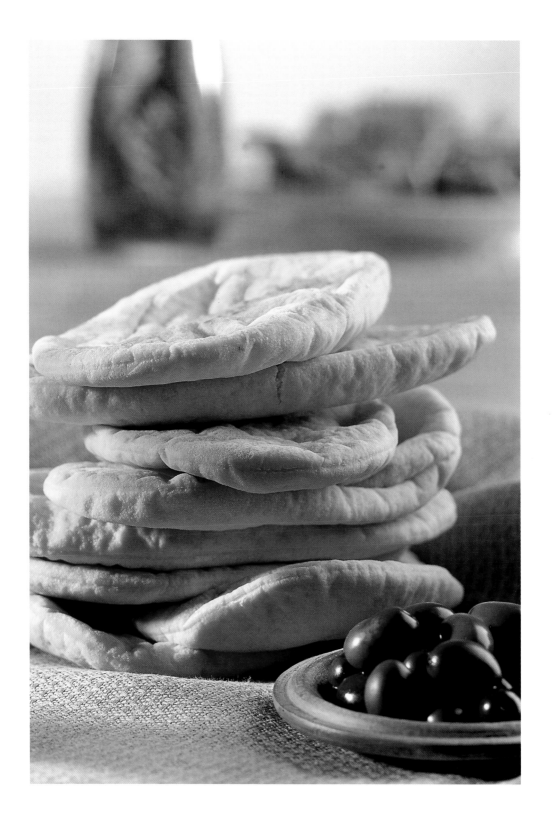

american corn bread

		ingredients
extremely easy		150 ml/5 fl oz hand-hot water TOPPING
1 small loaf	5 tbsp hand-hot milk 1 tbsp water	
	1 tbsp corn oil 1 tbsp medium cornmeal	
	280 g/10 oz strong white bread flour	
	100 g/3½ oz fine cornmeal	
5 minutes	1 tsp salt	
	1½ tsp light brown sugar	
	1 tsp easy-blend dried yeast	
about 1¾ hours		

Pour the water, milk and corn oil into the bread pan.

Sprinkle the flour over the liquid to cover, then sprinkle in the fine cornmeal. Place the salt and sugar in 2 corners of the pan. Indent the flour without exposing the liquid and add the yeast.

Set the bread machine to the quick setting, medium crust, and press start. About 5 minutes before baking begins (about 20 minutes from the start) add the topping. Brush the top of the dough with the water and carefully sprinkle with the medium cornmeal.

When the cycle has finished, turn out the bread to cool.

floury baps

		ingredients
very easy	140 ml/4½ fl oz hand-hot water	2 tsp caster sugar
	140 ml/4½ fl oz hand-hot milk	1 tsp easy-blend dried yeast
10 baps	450 g/1 lb strong white bread flour, plus extra for dusting	sunflower oil, for greasing
		milk, for glazing
2¼ hours	1½ tsp salt	
15–20 minutes		

Pour the water and milk into the bread pan. Sprinkle the flour over the liquid to cover. Place the salt and sugar in 2 corners of the pan. Indent the flour without exposing the liquid and add the yeast. Set the bread machine to the dough setting and press start.

Remove the finished dough from the pan. Knock back gently on a lightly floured surface. Divide it into 10 equal pieces. Place on a tray and cover with lightly oiled clingfilm. Uncover one by one and shape into balls, then roll out into 10-cm/4-inch-long ovals. Cover with lightly oiled clingfilm and set aside in a warm place for about 30 minutes to rise. Remove the clingfilm and gently press the centre of each bap to release any large air bubbles.

Brush the tops with milk and dust with flour. Bake on 2 oiled baking sheets in a preheated oven, 200°C/400°F/Gas Mark 6, for 15–20 minutes, until lightly browned. Cool slightly. Serve warm.

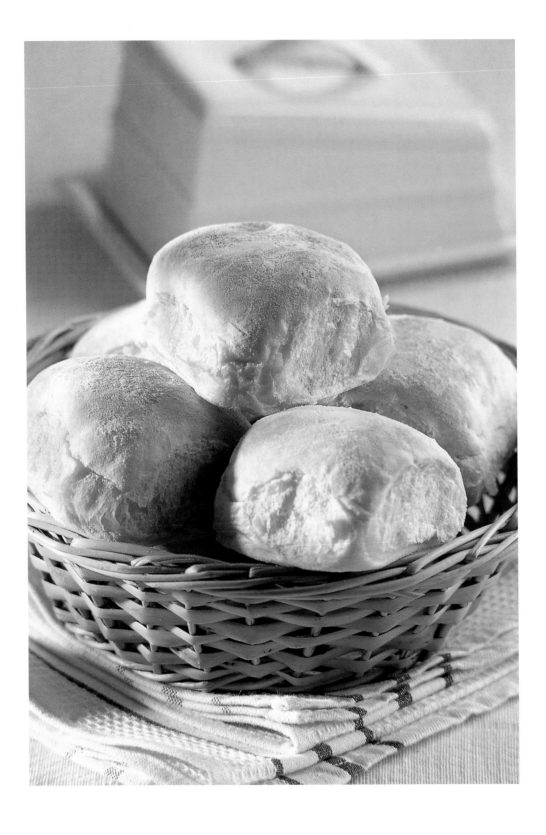

sesame breadsticks

very easy	
30 breadsticks	
2¼ hours	
15–20 minutes	

ingredients

200 ml/7 fl oz hand-hot water
3 tbsp olive oil, plus extra for greasing
  and brushing
350 g/12 oz strong white bread flour,
  plus extra for dusting

1½ tsp salt
1½ tsp easy-blend dried yeast
sesame seeds, for coating

Pour the water into the bread pan and add the olive oil. Sprinkle the flour over the liquid to cover. Place the salt in 1 corner. Indent the flour without exposing the liquid and add the yeast. Set the bread machine to the dough setting and press start.

Remove the finished dough from the pan. Knock back on a lightly floured surface and roll out into a 23 x 20-cm/9 x 8-inch rectangle. Cut the dough into 3 strips, each 20 cm/8 inches long, then cut each strip across into 10 equal pieces. Gently roll and stretch each piece into a stick about 30 cm/12 inches long. Roll in the sesame seeds to coat, then place on oiled baking sheets. Brush with oil, cover with clingfilm and set aside in a warm place for 15 minutes. Remove the clingfilm and bake the breadsticks in a preheated oven, 200°C/400°F/Gas Mark 6, for 10 minutes. Turn them over, return to the oven and bake for a further 5–10 minutes, until golden. Turn out the breadsticks to cool.

breakfast bakes

Life today is so rushed that most of us barely have time to grab a slice of toast in the morning – so these recipes are designed to provide an energy boost to get you going. They are as packed with flavour as they are with nutritional goodness. What could make a better start to the day than Orange Marmalade Loaf, unless it is Muesli Bread? The recipes also include some truly luxurious morning treats for weekends, holidays and special occasions. Impress overnight guests with home-made Petits Pains au Chocolat, or serve freshly griddled English Muffins for brunch.

muesli bread

		ingredients	
very easy	250 ml/8 fl oz hand-hot water	150 g/5½ oz unsweetened muesli	
	2 tbsp sunflower oil, plus extra	3 tbsp skimmed milk powder	
1 medium loaf	for greasing	1½ tsp salt	
	1 tbsp clear honey	1½ tsp easy-blend dried yeast	
	300 g/10½ oz strong white bread flour	70 g/2½ oz ready-to-eat dried	
	85 g/3 oz wholemeal bread flour, plus	apricots, chopped	
2¾–3 hours	extra for dusting		
30–35 minutes			

Put the water, sunflower oil and honey into the bread pan.

Sprinkle both types of flour over the liquid to cover, then sprinkle
in the muesli and skimmed milk powder. Place the salt in 1 corner
of the pan. Indent the flour without exposing the liquid and add
the yeast.

Set the bread machine to the dough setting and press start. Five
minutes before the end of kneading, add the dried apricots.

Remove the finished dough from the pan. Knock back gently on a
lightly floured surface, then shape into a round. Place the loaf on a
lightly oiled baking sheet. Cut a deep cross in the top with a sharp
knife. Cover with lightly oiled clingfilm and set aside in a warm
place for about 30–40 minutes to rise. Remove the clingfilm and
bake the loaf in a preheated oven, 200°C/400°F/Gas Mark 6, for
30–35 minutes, until golden. Turn out the bread to cool.

banana & orange bread

very easy	
1 medium loaf	
5 minutes	
about 3 hours	

ingredients

4 tbsp orange juice

200 ml/7 fl oz hand-hot buttermilk
  or water

2 medium ripe bananas or 1 large ripe
  banana, peeled and mashed

3 tbsp clear honey

500 g/1 lb 2 oz strong white bread
  flour, plus an extra 1–2 tbsp for
  sticky dough

1½ tbsp skimmed milk powder,
  optional

1 tsp salt

40 g/1½ oz butter, softened or diced

1 tsp easy-blend dried yeast

milk, for glazing, optional

Pour the orange juice and buttermilk into the bread pan.

Add the mashed bananas and honey. Sprinkle the flour over the liquid and fruit to cover. If using water, sprinkle the skimmed milk powder over the flour (it is not necessary if you have used buttermilk). Place the salt and butter in 2 corners of the bread pan. Indent the flour without exposing the liquid and add the yeast.

Set the bread machine to the basic setting, medium crust, and press start. If the dough looks very sticky towards the end of the first kneading, add a further 1–2 tablespoons of strong white bread flour. (The stickiness depends on the ripeness and size of the bananas.)

Just before the baking cycle starts (about 2 hours after the start), brush the top of the loaf with milk to glaze, if desired. Turn out the bread to cool.

bran & yogurt bread

		ingredients	

extremely easy		150 ml/5 fl oz hand-hot water
		125 ml/4 fl oz natural yogurt, at
		   room temperature
		1 tbsp sunflower oil
		1 tbsp treacle or golden syrup
		200 g/7 oz strong white bread flour
			150 g/5½ oz strong wholemeal
			   bread flour
			25 g/1 oz wheat bran
			1 tsp salt
			¾ tsp easy-blend dried yeast

1 small loaf			
5 minutes			
about 3 hours			

Pour the water into the bread pan and add the yogurt, sunflower oil and treacle.

Sprinkle both types of flour over the liquid to cover. Place the wheat bran and salt in 2 corners of the pan. Indent the flour without exposing the liquid and add the yeast.

Set the bread machine to the basic setting, medium crust, and press start.

When the cycle has finished, turn out the bread to cool.

mixed seed bread

extremely easy	
1 medium loaf	
5 minutes	
about 3 hours	

ingredients

300 ml/10 fl oz hand-hot water
1½ tbsp sunflower oil
2 tsp lemon juice
375 g/13 oz strong white bread flour
125 g/4½ oz rye flour
1½ tbsp skimmed milk powder
1½ tsp salt
1 tbsp light brown sugar
1 tsp caraway seeds

½ tsp poppy seeds
½ tsp sesame seeds
1 tsp easy-blend dried yeast

TOPPING
1 egg white
1 tbsp water
1 tbsp sunflower or pumpkin seeds

Pour the water into the bread pan and add the sunflower oil and lemon juice. Sprinkle both the flours over the liquid to cover, then sprinkle in the skimmed milk powder. Place the salt, sugar and seeds in 3 corners of the pan. Indent the flour without exposing the liquid and add the yeast.

Set the bread machine to the basic setting, medium crust, and press start.

For the topping, lightly beat the egg white with the water to make a glaze. Just before the baking cycle starts (about 2 hours after the start), brush the glaze over the loaf, then gently press the sunflower or pumpkin seeds all over the top.

When the cycle has finished, turn out the bread to cool.

spicy cinnamon bread

		ingredients	
	very easy	350 g/12 oz plain flour	55 g/2 oz butter
		1½ tsp baking powder	4 tbsp treacle
		¼ tsp salt	3 eggs, beaten lightly
	1 small loaf	1 tsp ground cinnamon	50 ml/2 fl oz milk
		½ tsp mixed spice	25 g/1 oz raisins
		½ tsp freshly grated nutmeg	55 g/2 oz dried apple rings, snipped
	25 minutes	½ tsp ground ginger	into pieces
	about 3 hours		

Sift the flour, baking powder, salt and spices into a mixing bowl and set aside.

Put the butter and treacle into a saucepan over a low heat, stirring constantly, until the butter has melted. Leave to cool slightly, then stir in the eggs, milk, raisins and apple pieces. Add the treacle mixture to the flour mixture and stir gently until combined.

Turn the mixture into the bread pan. Set the bread machine to the cake setting and press start.

When the cycle has finished, turn out the bread to cool.

orange marmalade loaf

		ingredients	
easy		150 ml/5 fl oz hand-hot water	1½ tsp easy-blend dried yeast
		150 ml/5 fl oz hand-hot milk	7 tbsp orange marmalade
1 medium loaf		2 tbsp sunflower oil, plus extra for greasing	TOPPING
		450 g/1 lb strong white bread flour, plus extra for dusting	1 egg yolk
2¾ hours		1½ tsp salt	1 tbsp milk
		1½ tsp sugar	1 tbsp caster sugar
25–30 minutes			1–2 tbsp crystallised orange peel

Pour the water and milk into the bread pan and add the oil. Sprinkle the flour over the liquid to cover. Put the salt and sugar in 2 corners. Indent the flour without exposing the liquid and add the yeast. Set the bread machine to the dough setting and press start.

Remove the dough from the bread pan. Knock back gently on a lightly floured surface. Roll out to a rectangle about 2 cm/¾ inch thick. Spread over the marmalade, leaving a 1-cm/½-inch border on one long side. Roll up like as Swiss roll and place seam-side down in a greased loaf tin. Cover with lightly oiled clingfilm and set aside in a warm place for about 45 minutes to rise. Remove the clingfilm.

For the topping, lightly beat the egg yolk, milk and sugar. Brush over the loaf. Score the top and arrange the orange peel over it. Bake in a preheated oven, 220°C/425°F/ Gas Mark 7, for 25–30 minutes, until golden. Turn out the bread to cool.

brioche

easy	
1 loaf	
3 hours	
40–45 minutes	

ingredients

2 eggs, at room temperature
2 tbsp hand-hot milk
225 g/8 oz strong white bread flour,
    plus extra for dusting
½ tsp salt
1 tbsp caster sugar
55 g/2 oz butter, melted

1½ tsp easy-blend dried yeast
sunflower oil, for greasing

GLAZE
1 egg yolk
1 tbsp milk or water

Lightly beat the eggs with the milk in a bowl, then pour into the bread pan. Sprinkle the flour over the liquid to cover. Place the salt, sugar and butter in 3 corners of the pan. Indent the flour without exposing the liquid and add the yeast. Set the bread machine to the dough setting and press start. With the lid shut, let the dough rise in the machine for an extra 30 minutes.

Remove the finished dough from the pan. Knock back gently on a floured surface. Slice off a quarter, wrap in oiled clingfilm and set aside. Oil a brioche mould. Knead the large piece of dough, shape into a ball, and place in the mould and indent the top. Unwrap the smaller piece and lightly knead into a pear shape. Place on top. Cover with clingfilm and set aside in a warm place for about 1 hour to rise. Remove the clingfilm. For the glaze, lightly beat the egg yolk with the milk. Brush over the top. Bake in a preheated oven, 220°C/425°F/Gas Mark 7, for 40–45 minutes, until golden.

english muffins

		ingredients	
very easy		350 ml/12 fl oz hand-hot milk	1 tsp caster sugar
		450 g/1 lb strong white bread flour, or	15 g/½ oz butter, softened or diced
10–11 muffins		225 g/8 oz strong white bread flour	1½ tsp easy-blend dried yeast
		plus 225 g/8 oz strong wholemeal	ground rice or rice flour, for dusting
		bread flour, plus extra for dusting	sunflower oil, for greasing
2 hours		1½ tsp salt	
35–40 minutes			

Pour the milk into the bread pan. Sprinkle the flour over the liquid to cover. Place the salt, sugar and butter in 3 corners of the pan. Indent the flour without exposing the liquid and add the yeast. Set the bread machine to the dough setting and press start.

Remove the finished dough from the bread pan. Knock back gently on a lightly floured surface, then roll out to 1 cm/½ inch thick. Stamp out rounds with a 7.5-cm/3-inch plain pastry cutter. Gather up the trimmings, knead together and leave to rest for 3–4 minutes. Re-roll and stamp out another 1–2 muffins.

Place the muffins on a dusted baking sheet. Dust the tops with ground rice. Cover with oiled clingfilm and set aside in a warm place for 20–25 minutes to rise. Remove the clingfilm. Lightly oil a griddle pan or heavy frying pan and heat well. Cook the muffins in batches, over a low heat, for 6–7 minutes on each side. Serve warm.

petits pains aux chocolat

		ingredients	
easy			

9 petits pains	125 ml/4 fl oz hand-hot water
	250 g/9 oz strong white bread flour
	2 tbsp skimmed milk powder
	½ tsp salt
	1 tbsp caster sugar
	140 g/5 oz butter, softened, plus extra
	  for greasing
		1½ tsp easy-blend dried yeast
		sunflower oil, for greasing
		225 g/8 oz plain chocolate, broken
		  into pieces
		
		GLAZE
		1 egg yolk, beaten
		1 tsp milk	

about 4 hours			
15 minutes			

Pour the water into the bread pan. Sprinkle in the flour and milk powder. Add the salt, sugar and 25 g/1 oz of the butter in 3 corners of the pan. Indent the flour then add the yeast. Set the machine at dough setting and press start. Shape the remaining butter into a rectangle 2 cm/¾ inch thick. Knock back the finished dough, shape into a ball and cut a cross in the centre. Roll out the edges around the cross. Place the butter in the centre and seal the edges over it. Roll out into a rectangle. With one short side towards you, fold the bottom-third up and the top-third down and seal. Wrap in clingfilm. Chill for 20 minutes. Repeat twice more, finally chilling for 30 minutes.

Roll out the dough into a large rectangle. Cut into 9 even pieces. Place chocolate pieces on each at a short end. Combine the egg yolk and milk, and brush over the edges. Roll up and seal. Place on oiled baking trays, seam-side down. Wrap and set aside for 30 minutes to rise. Brush with the remaining glaze. Bake in a preheated oven, 200°C/400°F/Gas Mark 6, for 15 minutes.

flaky almond pastries

		ingredients	
easy		**DANISH PASTRY**	**FILLING**
		5 tbsp hand-hot milk	1 tbsp butter
serves 12		2 eggs, one separated	85 g/3 oz caster sugar
		225 g/8 oz strong white bread flour,	85 g/3 oz ground almonds
		plus extra for dusting	2–3 drops almond essence
		$\frac{1}{2}$ tsp salt	1 small egg, beaten lightly
3½–4 hours		1 tbsp caster sugar	
		140 g/5 oz butter, softened	
		sunflower oil, for greasing	
15 minutes		1 tbsp water	
		flaked almonds, for sprinkling	

For the pastry, pour the milk into the bread pan and the egg. Add the flour, salt, sugar and 25 g/1 oz of the butter. Indent the flour and add yeast. Set the bread machine at dough setting. Press start. Shape the remaining butter into a 2-cm/³/₄-inch-thick rectangle. Roll the finished dough into a rectangle. Place the butter on one half, fold the other half over and seal. Roll out again into a rectangle. With one short side towards you, fold the top-third down and the bottom-third up, then seal. Wrap in clingfilm and chill for 15 minutes. Repeat twice more. Finally wrap and chill for 20 minutes.

For the filling, cream the butter with the sugar until pale. Add the almonds and essence. Mix to a paste with the beaten egg. Roll out the dough. Cut into 12 squares. Spread filling on half of each square. Brush the pastry edges with the white from the separated egg, fold over, and seal. Set aside on a baking sheet for 30 minutes to rise. Beat the egg yolk and water and glaze the pastries. Add the almonds. Bake in a preheated oven, 200°C/400°F/Gas Mark 6, for 15 minutes.

savoury breads

These substantial and flavour-packed
loaves are ideal for turning a snack into a
satisfying and nourishing lunch. They also
add the perfect touch to a family supper or
an informal dinner party. Herbs, spices,
cheese and nuts can all be easily
incorporated into the dough to create a
loaf that will really liven up a meal. Impress
your guests by choosing from international
favourites to match your main course. If
you are serving a curry, why not make some
Coriander and Garlic Naan? And what could
go better with pasta than Sun-dried
Tomato and Basil Ciabatta?

cheesy granary bread

		ingredients	
very easy		185 ml/6½ fl oz hand-hot water	1½ tsp easy-blend dried yeast
		1 egg, beaten lightly	85 g/3 oz dolcelatte cheese, diced
1 medium loaf		5 tbsp ricotta cheese, beaten	finely
		until smooth	85 g/3 oz freshly grated Emmenthal
		55 g/2 oz granary flour	cheese
2½ hours		400 g/14 oz strong white bread flour,	3 tbsp finely chopped fresh chives
		plus extra for dusting	sunflower oil, for greasing
		1 tsp salt	2 tbsp freshly grated Parmesan cheese
30–35 minutes		2 tsp sugar	

Pour the water into the bread pan and add the egg and ricotta.

Sprinkle both flours over the liquid to cover. Place the salt and sugar in 2 corners of the pan. Indent the flour without exposing the liquid and add the yeast. Set the bread machine to the dough setting and press start. Five minutes before the end of kneading, add the dolcelatte, Emmenthal and chives.

Remove the finished dough from the bread pan. Knock back gently on a lightly floured surface. Shape into a round loaf, about 20 cm/ 8 inches in diameter. Place on an oiled baking sheet, cover with lightly oiled clingfilm and set aside in a warm place for 40–45 minutes to rise.

Remove the clingfilm and sprinkle the Parmesan over the top of the loaf. Bake in a preheated oven, 200°C/400°F/Gas Mark 6, for 40–45 minutes, until golden. Turn out the bread to cool.

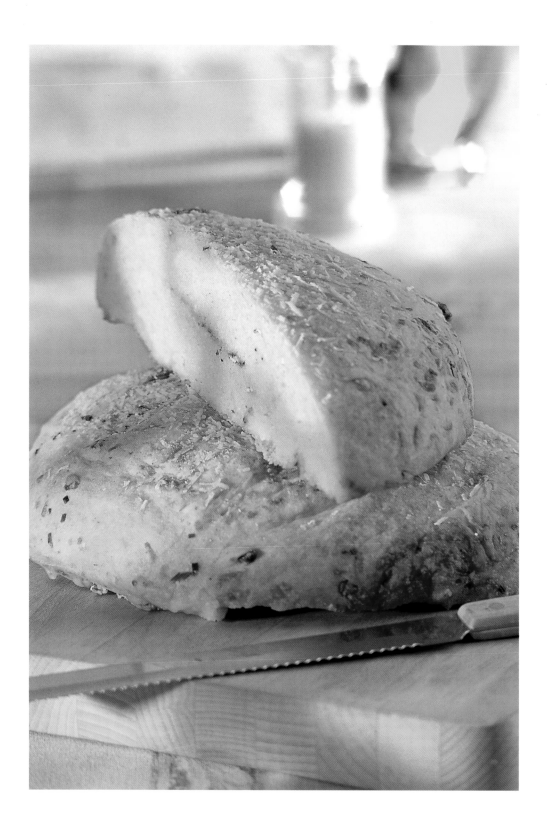

rosemary bread

		ingredients	
extremely easy	160 ml/5½ fl oz hand-hot water	1 tbsp finely chopped fresh rosemary
	2 eggs, beaten lightly	1½ tsp salt
1 medium loaf	4 tbsp olive oil	2 tsp sugar
	500g/1 lb 2 oz strong white bread flour	1 tsp easy-blend dried yeast
		115 g/4 oz dried figs, chopped roughly
10 minutes	2 tbsp skimmed milk powder	
about 3 hours		

Pour the water into the bread pan and add the eggs and olive oil.

Sprinkle the flour over the liquid to cover, then sprinkle in the skimmed milk powder and the rosemary. Place the salt and sugar in 2 corners of the pan. Indent the flour without exposing the liquid and add the yeast.

Set the bread machine to the basic setting, medium crust, and press start. Five minutes before the end of kneading, add the figs.

When the cycle has finished, turn out the bread to cool.

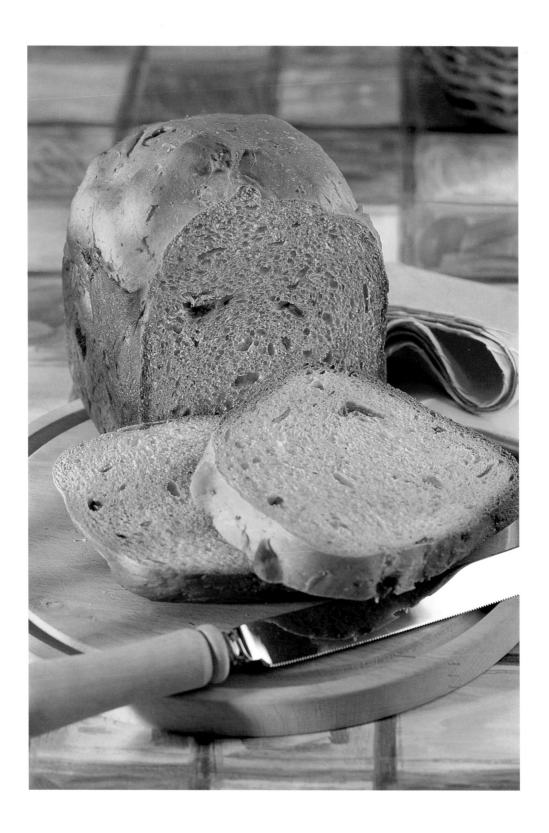

greek olive & feta bread

		ingredients	
very easy		210 ml/7½ fl oz hand-hot water	1½ tsp sugar
		375 g/13 oz strong white bread flour,	1 tsp easy-blend dried yeast
1 medium loaf		plus extra for dusting	55 g/2 oz stoned black olives, chopped
		1 tbsp skimmed milk powder	55 g/2 oz feta cheese, crumbled
		1 tsp salt	olive oil, for brushing and greasing
2½ hours			herbs for sprinkling
35–40 minutes			

Pour the water into the bread pan. Sprinkle the flour over the liquid to cover, then sprinkle in the skimmed milk powder. Place the salt and sugar in 2 corners of the pan. Indent the flour without exposing the liquid and add the yeast.

Set the bread machine to the dough setting. Five minutes before the end of kneading, add the olives and feta.

Remove the finished dough from the bread pan. Gently knock back the dough on a lightly floured surface. Shape the dough into a round loaf 20 cm/8 inches in diameter. Place it in an oiled 20-cm/8-inch-diameter round cake tin, cover with oiled clingfilm and set aside in a warm place for 40–45 minutes to rise.

Remove the clingfilm and brush the top of the loaf with olive oil and sprinkle with herbs. Bake in a preheated oven, 200°C/400°F/Gas Mark 6, for 35-40 minutes, until golden. Turn out the bread to cool.

fresh herb cottage loaf

		ingredients	
very easy		300 ml/10 fl oz hand-hot water	2 tbsp chopped fresh chives
		450 g/1 lb strong white bread flour,	1 tbsp chopped fresh thyme
1 loaf		plus extra for dusting	sunflower oil, for greasing
		1½ tsp salt	
		1½ tsp sugar	GLAZE
2½ hours		1½ tsp easy-blend dried yeast	1 tbsp water
		2 tbsp chopped fresh parsley	1 tbsp salt
30–35 minutes			

Pour the water into the bread pan. Sprinkle the flour over the liquid to cover. Place the salt and sugar in 2 corners of the pan. Indent the flour without exposing the liquid and add the yeast. Set the bread machine to the dough setting. Five minutes before the end of kneading, add all the herbs.

Remove the finished dough from the pan. Knock back on a gently floured surface, then cut off one-third of the dough. Shape each piece into a ball. Cover with oiled clingfilm and set aside in a warm place for 30 minutes to rise. Unwrap the dough and cut a cross in the top of the larger piece. Brush with water and place the smaller piece on top. Make a hole through the centre of both balls of dough. Cover and set aside in a warm place for 10 minutes to rise.

Mix the water and salt and glaze the loaf. Slash around the loaf and dust with flour. Bake in a preheated oven, 220°C/425°F/Gas Mark 7, for 30–35 minutes, until golden. Turn out to cool.

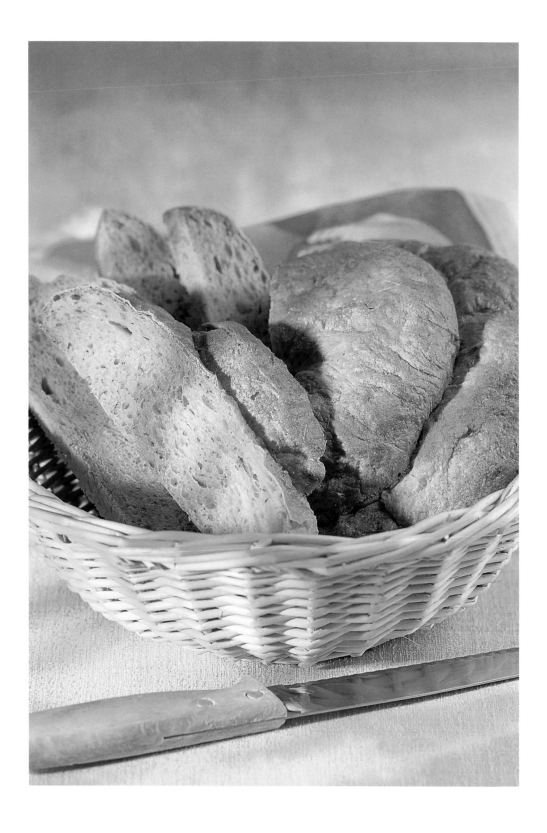

walnut bread

		ingredients	
extremely easy		250 ml/8 fl oz hand-hot water	1½ tsp dried marjoram
		5 tsp sunflower oil	1½ tsp dried thyme
1 medium loaf		1½ tsp walnut oil	1½ tsp salt
		1½ tsp basil in oil, drained	2¼ tbsp sugar
		350 g/12 oz strong white bread flour	1¼ tsp easy-blend dried yeast
10 minutes		2½ tbsp skimmed milk powder	70 g/2½ oz walnuts, chopped and
			whole walnuts for garnish
about 3 hours			

Pour the water into the bread pan and add the sunflower oil, walnut oil and basil.

Sprinkle the flour over the liquid to cover, then sprinkle in the skimmed milk powder and dried herbs. Place the salt and sugar in 2 corners of the pan. Indent the flour without exposing the liquid and add the yeast.

Set the bread machine to the basic setting, medium crust. Five minutes before the end of kneading add the chopped walnuts. Before the baking cycle starts add the whole walnuts to the top, if required.

When the cycle has finished, turn out the bread to cool.

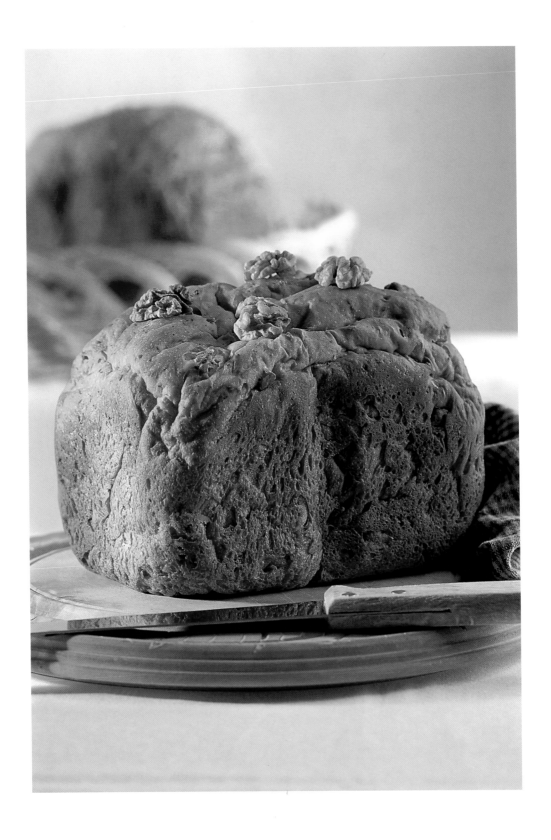

finnish rye & caraway bread

		ingredients	
extremely easy		350 ml/12 fl oz hand-hot water	75 g/2¾ oz dried breadcrumbs
		2 tbsp sunflower oil	3 tbsp oat bran
1 medium loaf		2½ tbsp treacle	1½ tsp salt
		250 g/9 oz strong white bread flour	1½ tbsp cocoa powder
		140 g/5 oz rye flour	2 tsp caraway seeds
		85 g/3 oz wholemeal flour	½ tsp easy-blend dried yeast
10 minutes			
about 3½ hours			

Pour the water into the bread pan and add the oil and treacle.

Sprinkle all 3 types of flour over the liquid to cover, then sprinkle in the breadcrumbs and bran. Place the salt, cocoa powder and caraway seeds in 3 corners of the pan. Indent the flour without exposing the liquid and add the yeast.

Set the bread machine to the wholemeal setting, medium crust, and press start.

When the cycle has finished, turn out the bread to cool.

sun-dried tomato
& basil ciabatta

		ingredients	
easy		**ITALIAN SPONGE**	325 g/11½ oz strong white bread
		200 ml/7 fl oz hand-hot water	flour, plus extra for dusting
2 loaves		175 g/6 oz strong white bread flour	1½ tsp salt
		½ tsp easy-blend dried yeast	½ tsp sugar
			¼ tsp easy-blend dried yeast
		DOUGH	40 g/1½ oz drained sun-dried
14 hours		200 ml/7 fl oz hand-hot water	tomatoes in oil, chopped roughly,
		2 tbsp olive oil, plus extra for greasing	additional for topping if required
		2 tbsp milk	2 tbsp shredded fresh basil
25–30 minutes			

For the sponge, pour the water into the bread pan. Sprinkle the flour over the liquid to cover. Indent the flour without exposing the liquid and add the yeast. Set the bread machine to the dough setting and press start. After 5 minutes, switch off the machine and leave for 12 hours. For the dough, pour the water into the bread pan with the Italian sponge. Add the oil and milk. Sprinkle the flour over the liquid to cover. Place the salt and sugar in 2 corners of the pan. Indent the flour without exposing the liquid and add the yeast. Set the machine to the dough setting. Five minutes before the end of kneading, add the sun-dried tomatoes and basil.

Transfer the finished dough to a bowl, cover with clingfilm and set aside in a warm place for about 1 hour to rise. Turn out and shape into two rectangular loaves about 2.5 cm/1 inch thick. Dust with flour and set aside, uncovered, in a warm place for 30 minutes to rise. Add a topping if required. Bake on oiled baking sheets in a preheated oven, 220°C/425°F/Gas Mark 7, for 25–30 minutes, until golden.

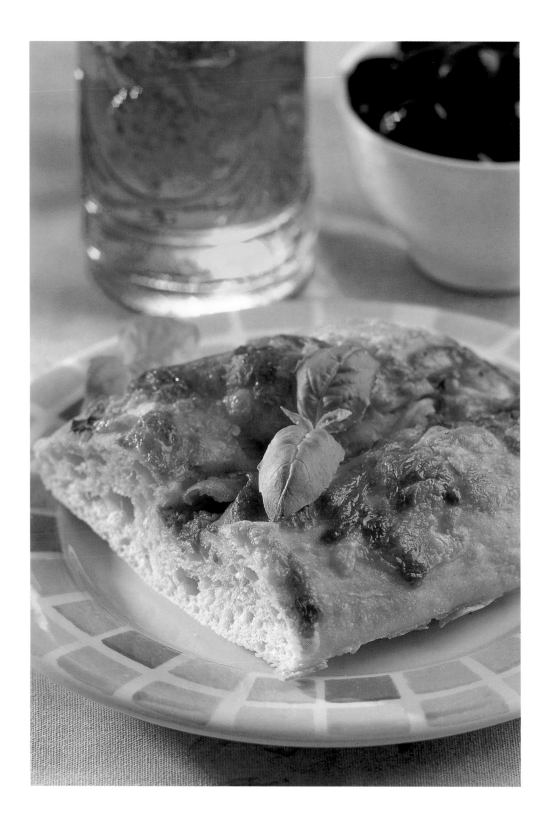

coriander & garlic naan

		ingredients	
easy		100 ml/3½ fl oz hand-hot water	1 tbsp ghee or butter, melted, plus
		4 tbsp natural yogurt	extra for brushing
3 flatbreads		280 g/10 oz strong white bread flour	1 tsp easy-blend dried yeast
		1 garlic clove, chopped finely	sunflower oil, for greasing
		1 tsp ground coriander	1 tsp black onion seeds
1¾ hours		1 tsp salt	1 tbsp chopped fresh coriander
		2 tsp clear honey	
6–8 minutes			

Pour the water into the bread pan and add the yogurt. Sprinkle the flour over the liquid to cover, then sprinkle in the garlic and ground coriander. Place the salt, honey and melted ghee in 3 corners of the pan. Indent the flour without exposing the liquid and add the yeast. Set the bread machine to the dough setting or pizza dough setting and press start.

Place 3 baking sheets in the oven to preheat to 240°C/475°F/Gas Mark 9. Remove the finished dough from the bread pan. Knock back on a lightly floured surface and divide into 3 pieces. Shape each piece into a ball and cover 2 of them with oiled clingfilm. Roll the uncovered piece into a teardrop shape about 8 mm/⅜ inch thick. Cover with oiled clingfilm, then roll out the other pieces of dough in turn. Place on the hot baking sheets and sprinkle with the onion seeds and chopped coriander. Bake for about 5 minutes, until puffed up. Grill and brush with melted ghee and serve warm.

light lunches & suppers

Home-made pizza is a special treat and, with a bread machine, making perfect pizza dough is simplicity itself. This chapter includes recipes for different kinds of dough. It's up to you whether you make thin-crust or thick-crust, large or individual pizzas – there is also a recipe for calzone, a sort of inside-out pizza. The recipes here include a selection of toppings, but you can substitute your favourite ingredients for tailor-made pizzas to suit all the family. This chapter also provides recipes for focaccia and the Provençal recipe, Pissaladière.

pepperoni & red onion pizza

easy	
2 x 25-cm/ 10-inch pizzas	
about 2 hours	
20–30 minutes	

ingredients

DOUGH
225 ml/7½ fl oz hand-hot water
15 g/½ oz butter, melted
325 g/11½ oz strong white bread
  flour, plus extra for dusting
1 tsp salt
2 tbsp sugar
1 tsp easy-blend dried yeast
olive oil, for greasing

TOPPING
4 tbsp sun-dried tomato paste
4 tomatoes, skinned and sliced thinly
2 red onions, chopped finely
4 slices prosciutto, shredded
12 slices pepperoni sausage
12 black olives
salt
¾ tsp herbes de Provence
55 g/2 oz mozzarella cheese, grated
olive oil, for drizzling

Pour the water into the bread pan and add the melted butter. Sprinkle the flour over the liquid to cover. Place the salt and sugar in 2 corners of the pan. Indent the flour without exposing the liquid and add the yeast. Set the bread machine to the pizza dough or dough setting and press start.

Remove the finished dough from the pan. Knock back gently on a lightly floured surface and divide in half. Roll out each piece of dough into a 25-cm/10-inch round and place on greased pizza pans or baking sheets. Push up the edges slightly. Cover with lightly oiled clingfilm and set aside to rest for 15 minutes.

For the topping, spread the sun-dried tomato paste evenly over each round. Arrange the tomato slices on top. Sprinkle over the onion, prosciutto, pepperoni and olives. Add the seasoning, herbs and grated cheese and drizzle with olive oil. Bake in a preheated oven, 220°C/425°F/Gas Mark 7, for 20–30 minutes, until sizzling.

spinach, ricotta & pine kernel pizza

easy	
2 x 30-cm/ 12-inch pizzas	
about 2 hours	
20–30 minutes	

ingredients

DOUGH
300 ml/10 fl oz hand-hot water
2 tbsp olive oil, plus extra for greasing
225 g/8 oz strong white bread flour, plus extra for dusting
225 g/8 oz strong wholemeal bread flour
1½ tsp salt
½ tsp sugar
1 tsp easy-blend dried yeast

TOPPING
2 tbsp olive oil, plus extra for drizzling
1 onion, sliced thinly
350 g/12 oz spinach, washed and dried
6 tbsp ricotta cheese
½ tsp freshly grated nutmeg
2 tbsp pine kernels
salt and pepper
115 g/4 oz Fontina cheese, sliced thinly

Pour the water into the bread pan and add the olive oil. Sprinkle both flours over the liquid to cover. Add the salt and sugar. Indent the flour without exposing the liquid and add the yeast. Set the machine to the pizza dough or dough setting and press start.

Remove the finished dough from the pan. Knock back gently on a lightly floured surface and divide in half. Roll out each piece of dough into a 30-cm/12-inch round and place on greased pizza pans or baking sheets. Push up the edges slightly. Cover with lightly oiled clingfilm and set aside to rest for 15 minutes.

Heat the oil in a pan. Add the onion and cook until soft, then add the spinach. Spread the ricotta cheese evenly over the pizza bases, then the onion mixture. Sprinkle with nutmeg and pine kernels and season to taste. Top with the cheese and drizzle with olive oil. Bake in a preheated oven, 220°C/425°F/Gas Mark 7, for 20–30 minutes, until sizzling.

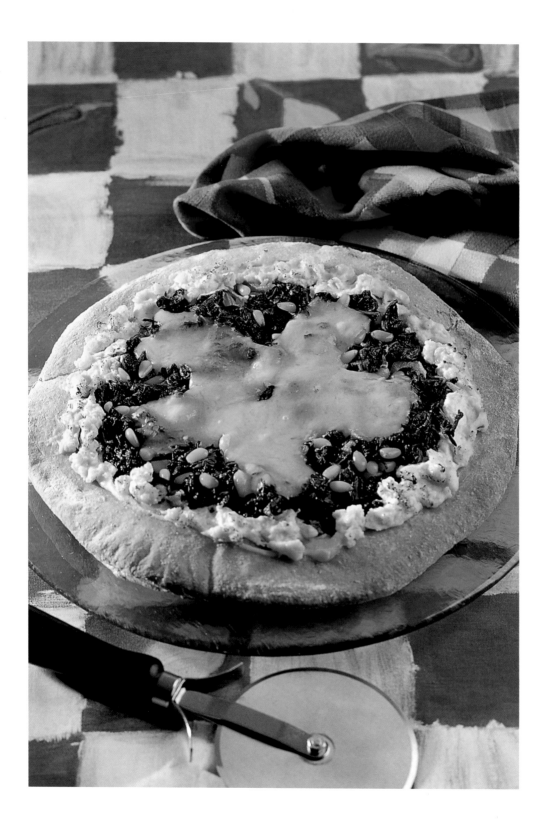

chargrilled vegetable calzone

		ingredients	
easy	**DOUGH**	2 baby aubergines, quartered
	140 ml/4½ fl oz hand-hot water	lengthways
	2 tbsp olive oil, plus extra for greasing	2 courgettes, halved lengthways
2 calzones	and brushing	1 small red pepper, deseeded and
	225 g/8 oz strong white bread flour	quartered lengthways
	1 tsp salt	1 small orange pepper, deseeded and
about	½ tsp sugar	quartered lengthways
2½ hours	1 tsp easy-blend dried yeast	4 tbsp olive oil
		1 tbsp balsamic vinegar
	FILLING	1 tbsp chopped fresh parsley
20–30	1 red onion, cut into wedges	salt and pepper
minutes	2 garlic cloves, skin left on	85 g/3 oz goat's cheese, diced

Pour the water into the bread pan and add the olive oil. Sprinkle the flour over the liquid to cover. Add the salt and sugar. Indent the flour without exposing the liquid and add the yeast. Set the machine to the pizza dough or dough setting and press start. Remove the dough from the pan. Knock back gently on a lightly floured surface and divide in half. Roll out each piece into a round about 5 mm/¼ inch thick and place on a baking sheet. Cover with lightly oiled clingfilm and set aside to rest for 15 minutes.

Place the vegetables in a roasting tin. Combine the oil, vinegar, parsley and seasoning and pour over the top. Roast for about 15 minutes, at 200°C/400°F/Gas Mark 6, turning once. Cool. Peel off the garlic and pepper skins and cover half of each dough round with vegetables and the goat's cheese, leaving a border. Brush the edges with water and fold the halves over and seal. Brush with olive oil and bake in a preheated oven, 220°C/425°F/Gas Mark 7, for 20–30 minutes, until golden.

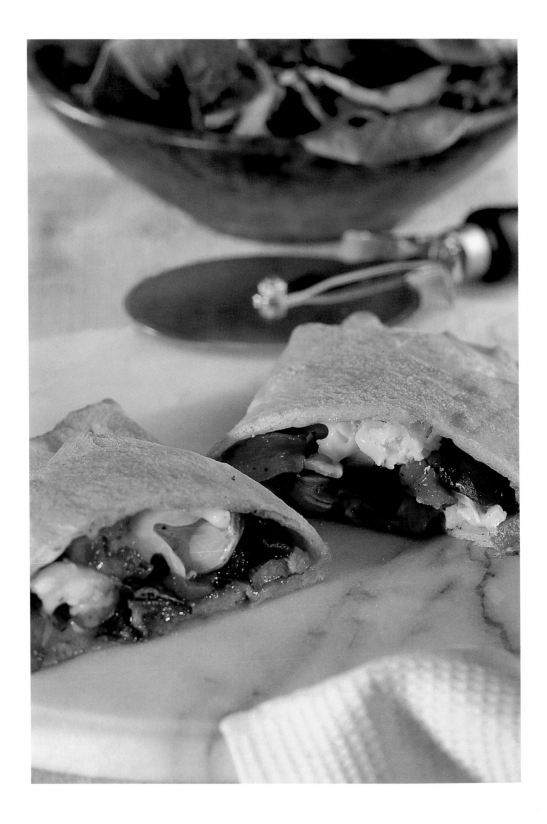

mozzarella &
rosemary focaccia

		ingredients
easy		
1 loaf	210 ml/7½ fl oz hand-hot water	TOPPING
	1 tbsp olive oil, plus extra for greasing	2 tbsp olive oil
	350 g/12 oz strong white bread flour,	fresh rosemary sprigs
	plus extra for dusting	coarse sea salt
2¼ hours	½ tsp salt	
	1 tsp sugar	
	1 tsp easy-blend dried yeast	
20–25 minutes	140 g/5 oz mozzarella cheese, grated	

Pour the water into the bread pan and add the oil. Sprinkle the flour over the liquid to cover. Place the salt and sugar in 2 corners of the pan. Indent the flour without exposing the liquid and add the yeast. Set the bread machine to the pizza dough or dough setting and press start.

Remove the finished dough from the pan. Knock back and gently flatten on a floured surface. Sprinkle over the mozzarella and knead. Shape into a ball, flatten slightly, then roll out into a 25-cm/10-inch round. Place in a lightly oiled cake tin. Cover with lightly oiled clingfilm and set aside in a warm place for 20 minutes to rise. Remove the clingfilm. Make indentations in the surface of the dough. Cover again and set aside in a warm place to rise for 15 minutes. Remove the clingfilm. Drizzle over the olive oil, then sprinkle with the rosemary sprigs and coarse sea salt. Bake in a preheated oven, 200°C/400°F/Gas Mark 6, for 20–25 minutes, until golden. Turn out to cool slightly. Serve warm.

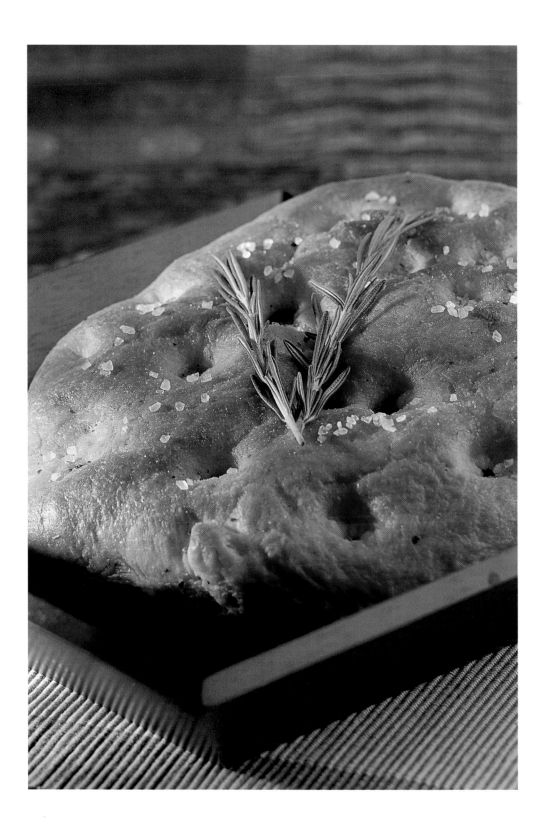

pissaladière

		ingredients	
easy		100 ml/3½ fl oz hand-hot water	TOPPING
		1 egg, beaten lightly	3 tsp olive oil
serves 6		225 g/8 oz strong white bread flour,	500 g/1 lb 2 oz red onions, sliced thinly
		plus extra for dusting	2 garlic cloves, chopped finely
		1 tsp salt	2 tsp caster sugar
		25 g/1 oz butter, softened or diced	1½ tbsp balsamic vinegar
1¾ hours		1 tsp easy-blend dried yeast	salt and pepper
		olive oil, for greasing	100 g/3½ oz canned anchovy
			fillets, drained
25–30 minutes			12 black olives
			1 tsp dried marjoram

Pour the water into the bread pan and add the egg. Sprinkle the flour over the liquid to cover. Place the salt and butter in 2 corners of the pan. Indent the flour without exposing the liquid and add the yeast. Set the bread machine to the pizza dough or dough setting and press start. Remove the dough from the pan.

For the topping, heat the oil. Add the onions and garlic. Cook over a low heat for 30 minutes. Add the sugar, vinegar and seasoning. Cook, stirring for 5 minutes, then set aside to cool.

Knock back the dough gently on a lightly floured surface, then roll out into a 30 x 23-cm/12 x 9-inch rectangle. Place in a Swiss roll tin. Spread the onion mixture over the base of the dough. Arrange the anchovy fillets on top with the olives. Sprinkle with marjoram. Cover with oiled clingfilm and set aside in a warm place for 10–15 minutes. Remove the clingfilm and bake in a preheated oven, 200°C/400°F/Gas Mark 6, for 25–30 minutes.

coffee break & teatime treats

These delightful specialities are absurdly easy to make using a bread machine, which produces results to rival a professional pâtissier. Bake simple sweet breads in the machine or push the boat out and make an elegant, twisted loaf of Cornish Saffron Bread. The bread machine is perfect for cake-making, too. Use it to mix yeast doughs to perfection before cooking in a mould or tin or shaping into buns. Give yourself a mid-morning pick-me-up, take a well-deserved break with afternoon tea or simply indulge your sweet tooth at any time of day.

malted fruit loaf

extremely easy	
1 medium loaf	
10 minutes	
about 3 hours	

ingredients

225 ml/7½ fl oz hand-hot water	350 g/12 oz plain flour
2 tsp sunflower oil	1 tsp salt
2 tbsp malt extract	1 tsp easy-blend dried yeast
1½ tbsp treacle	140 g/5 oz sultanas

Pour the water into the bread pan and add the sunflower oil, malt extract and treacle.

Sprinkle the flour over the liquid to cover. Place the salt in 1 corner of the pan. Indent the flour without exposing the liquid and add the yeast.

Set the bread machine to basic setting, medium crust. Five minutes before the end of kneading, add the sultanas.

When the cycle has finished, turn out the bread to cool.

pecan honey tea bread

	ingredients	
extremely easy	125 ml/4 fl oz hand-hot milk	¾ tsp salt
	175 ml/6 fl oz mandarin or orange	40 g/1½ oz butter, softened or diced
1 medium loaf	yogurt, at room temperature	1½ tbsp yeast
	3 tbsp clear honey	40 g/1½ oz pecan nuts, chopped
10 minutes	500 g/1 lb 2 oz strong white	1 tbsp grated orange rind, optional
	bread flour	
about 3 hours		

Pour the milk into the bread pan and add the yogurt and honey.

Sprinkle the flour over the liquid to cover. Place the salt and butter in 2 corners of the pan. Indent the flour without exposing the liquid and add the yeast.

Set the bread machine to the basic setting, medium crust. Five minutes before the end of kneading, add the pecan nuts and the orange rind, if desired.

When the cycle has finished, turn out the bread to cool.

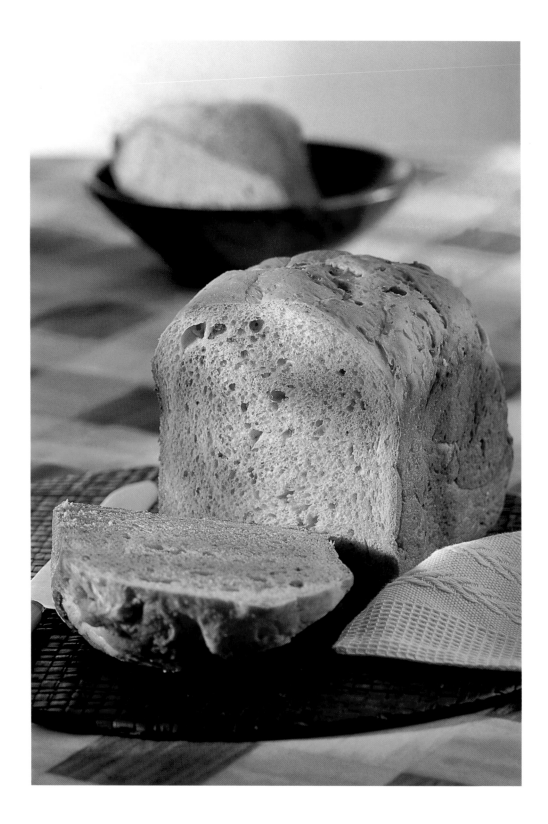

cornish saffron bread

		ingredients	
easy		1 tsp saffron threads	55 g/2 oz butter, melted
		200 ml/7 fl oz milk	1 tsp easy-blend dried yeast
1 loaf		2 eggs, beaten lightly	sunflower oil, for greasing
		500 g/1 lb 2 oz strong white bread flour, plus extra for dusting	GLAZE
2¾ hours		½ tsp salt	1–2 tbsp clear honey
		4 tbsp caster sugar	
30–35 minutes			

Place the saffron threads in a small bowl. Heat 5 tablespoons of the milk in a small saucepan, pour it over the saffron and set aside for at least 30 minutes. Pour the saffron milk and remaining milk into the bread pan and add the eggs. Sprinkle the flour over the liquid to cover. Place the salt, sugar and butter in 3 corners of the pan. Indent the flour without exposing the liquid and add the yeast. Set the bread machine to the dough setting and press start.

Remove the finished dough from the pan. Knock back gently on a floured surface, then divide it into 2 long ropes and twist together. Place on a greased baking sheet, cover with oiled clingfilm and set aside in a warm place for about 1 hour to rise. Heat the honey for the glaze in a small pan until runny. Remove the clingfilm and brush over the loaf. Bake in a preheated oven, 190°C/375°F/Gas Mark 5, for 20 minutes. Lower to 180°C/350°F/Gas Mark 4 and bake for a further 10–15 minutes, until golden. Turn out to cool.

hungarian coffee cake

		ingredients

		ingredients	
easy		5 tbsp strong black coffee	85 g/3 oz caster sugar
		2 tbsp brandy	2 tsp easy-blend dried yeast
1 loaf		1 cinnamon stick	85 g/3 oz butter, melted, plus
		115 g/4 oz raisins	extra for greasing
		2 tbsp hand-hot milk	sunflower oil, for greasing
2½ hours		3 eggs	2 egg whites
		500 g/1 lb 2 oz strong white	icing sugar, for dusting
		bread flour	
55–60 minutes		½ tsp salt	

Pour the coffee into a small pan. Add the brandy and cinnamon stick and heat. Add the raisins. Set aside for 30 minutes. Pour the milk into the bread pan and strain in the coffee mixture. Discard the cinnamon stick and reserve the raisins. Add the eggs. Sprinkle the flour over the liquid to cover. Add the salt and sugar. Indent the flour without exposing the liquid and add the yeast. Set the machine to the dough setting and press start. Add the butter in thirds at 5-minute intervals from the start.

Turn out the finished dough into a bowl. Knead in the reserved raisins. Grease a large brioche mould with butter. Whisk the egg whites to soft peaks. Gradually fold them into the dough. Spoon the dough into the brioche mould, cover with oiled clingfilm and set aside in a warm place for 1¼–1½ hours to rise. Remove the clingfilm and bake in a preheated oven, 190°C/375°F/Gas Mark 5, for 55–60 minutes. Cool, then dust with icing sugar before serving.

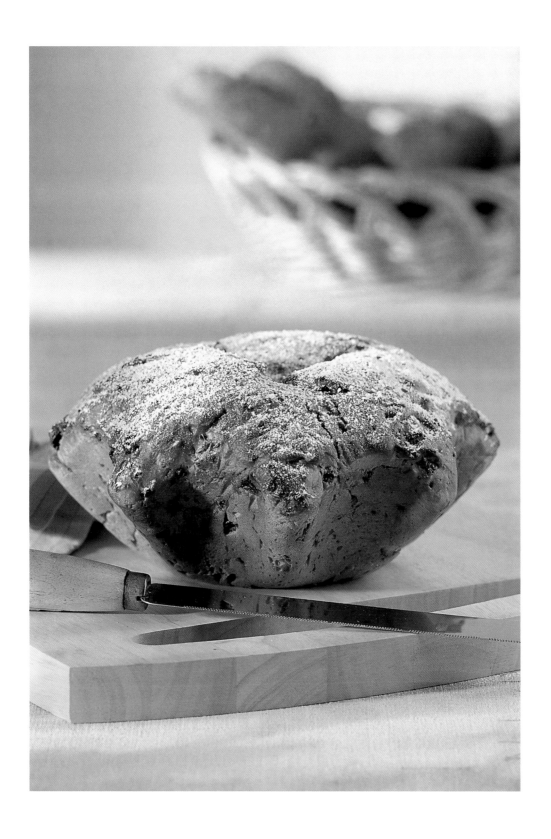

apple & walnut streusel cake

easy	**ingredients**
one 25-cm/ 10-inch cake	
2¼ hours	
30 minutes	

100 ml/3½ fl oz hand-hot milk	TOPPING
1 egg, beaten lightly	115 g/4 oz plain flour
250 g/9 oz strong white bread flour, plus extra for dusting	55 g/2 oz butter, diced
½ tsp salt	55 g/2 oz walnuts, chopped finely
3 tbsp caster sugar	4 tbsp caster sugar
25 g/1 oz butter, melted	1 tsp ground cinnamon
1 tsp easy-blend dried yeast	4 eating apples
sunflower oil, for greasing	2 tbsp lemon juice

Pour the milk into the bread pan and add the egg. Sprinkle the flour over the liquid to cover. Add the salt, sugar and butter. Indent the flour without exposing the liquid and add the yeast. Set the bread machine to the dough setting and press start. For the topping, sift the flour into a bowl and add the butter. Rub in. Stir in the walnuts, sugar and cinnamon. Set aside.

Lightly grease a 25-cm/10-inch springform cake tin. Remove the finished dough from the pan. Knock back gently on a floured surface, then roll out to fit the tin. Peel, core and thinly slice the apples. Toss them in the lemon juice and arrange on top of the dough. Sprinkle the nut topping over them. Cover the cake with lightly oiled clingfilm and set aside in a warm place for 25–30 minutes to rise. Remove the clingfilm and bake the cake in a preheated oven, 190°C/375°F/Gas Mark 5, for about 30 minutes, until golden. Leave in the tin to cool for 5 minutes, then turn out.

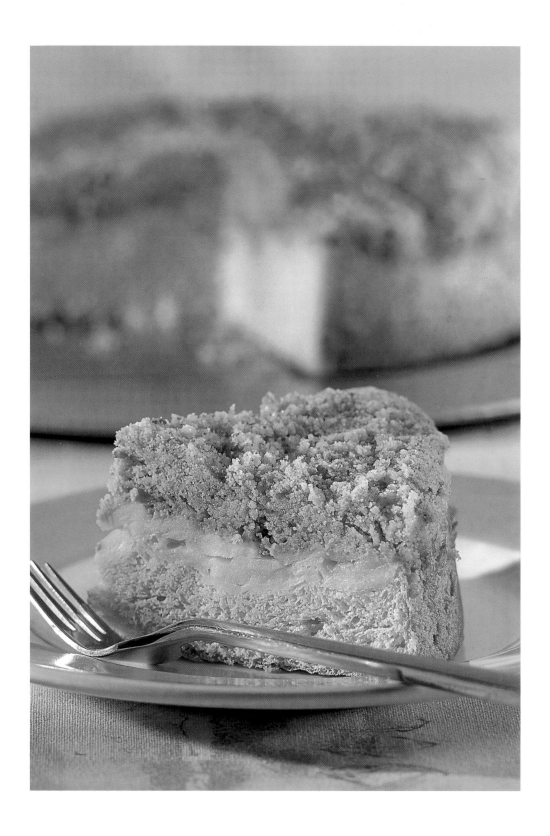

sticky apricot &
cinnamon buns

		ingredients	
	easy	225 ml/7½ fl oz hand-hot milk	FILLING
		1 egg, beaten lightly	25 g/1 oz butter, melted
	12 buns	500 g/1 lb 2 oz strong white bread	115 g/4 oz ready-to-eat dried
		flour, plus extra for dusting	apricots, chopped
		½ tsp salt	55 g/2 oz sultanas
		85 g/3 oz caster sugar	2 tbsp light brown sugar
	2½ hours	55 g/2 oz butter, softened or diced	1½ tsp ground cinnamon
		1 tsp easy-blend dried yeast	
		sunflower oil, for greasing	GLAZE
			4 tbsp water
	20 minutes		4 tbsp caster sugar
			1 tsp Amaretto liqueur

Pour the milk into the bread pan and add the egg. Sprinkle the flour over the liquid to cover. Add the salt, sugar and butter. Indent the flour without exposing the liquid and add the yeast. Set the machine to the dough setting and press start. Remove the finished dough from the pan. Knock back on a floured surface. Roll out into a 30-cm/12-inch square. For the filling, brush the dough with the butter, then sprinkle over the apricots, sultanas, sugar and cinnamon, leaving a border on one edge. Roll up towards the border, and seal. Cut into 12 slices. Place in a 23-cm/9-inch cake tin, with the cut sides upwards. Cover with clingfilm and set aside in a warm place for about 45 minutes to rise. Remove the clingfilm and bake in a preheated oven, 200°C/400°F/Gas Mark 6, for about 20 minutes. Cool for 5 minutes, then turn out.

For the glaze bring the water and sugar to the boil in a small pan, stirring constantly. Boil for 1½–2 minutes, not stirring, until syrupy. Stir in the liqueur and brush over the buns. Serve warm or cold.

devonshire splits

		ingredients	
easy		150 ml/5 fl oz hand-hot milk	FILLING
		225 g/8 oz strong white bread flour,	strawberry jam
8 buns		plus extra for dusting	double cream, whipped stiffly, or
		½ tsp salt	clotted cream
		2 tbsp caster sugar	
3 hours		1 tsp easy-blend dried yeast	
		sunflower oil, for greasing	
		icing sugar, for dusting	
15 minutes			

Pour the milk into the pan. Sprinkle the flour over the liquid to cover. Place the salt and sugar in 2 corners of the pan. Indent the flour without exposing the liquid and add the yeast. Set the bread machine to the dough setting and press start.

Remove the finished dough from the pan. Knock back gently on a lightly floured surface. Divide into 8 equal pieces and shape each one into a ball. Place on 2 lightly greased baking sheets and flatten the tops slightly. Cover with lightly oiled clingfilm and set aside in a warm place for about 45 minutes to rise.

Remove the clingfilm and bake in a preheated oven, 220°C/425°F/ Gas Mark 7, for about 15 minutes, until golden. Turn out to cool completely.

When the buns are cold, cut them open and fill with strawberry jam and cream. Dust with icing sugar and serve.

index